This dragon book belongs to:

....

Teach Your Dragon To Follow Instructions
My Dragon Books - Volume 20
Written by Steve Herman

ISBN: 978-1948040600 (paperback)
ISBN: 978-1948040617 (hardcover)

www.MyDragonBooks.com

First Edition: November 2018

10 9 8 7 6 5 4 3 2 1

Teach Your Dragon To Follow Instructions

My Dragon Books - Volume 20

Steve Herman

His name is Diggory Doo,
and he's thoughtful and he's kind,
But it was quite a challenge
training Diggory Doo to mind.

Once Diggory Doo decided he would like to learn to bake, Mother shared her recipe for how to make a cake.

Mother said, "Before you start, be sure to wash your hands, Then gather your ingredients and use the proper pans."

When Diggory's cake was finished,
it looked good, without a doubt,

But when I took a bite of it, I had to spit it out!

I said, "This cake is awful!"
He replied, "It's not my fault!"

"When I ran out of sugar, I had to substitute SALT."

Though he saw there were instructions
Diggory didn't read 'em.
He said, "I know just what to do;
I don't think I'll need 'em."

When Diggory Doo had finished,
I saw he wore a frown –
He cried, "This plane is not quite right;
the wings are upside down!"

Miss Matthews teaches math;
she shows us what to do
Whenever we have homework
(and she's very patient, too!)

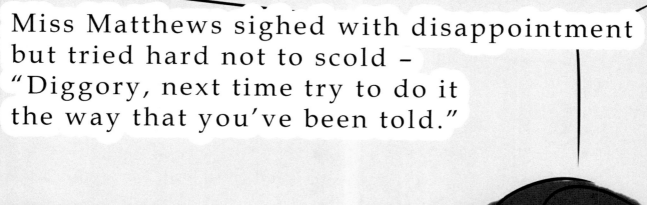

Miss Matthews sighed with disappointment but tried hard not to scold – "Diggory, next time try to do it the way that you've been told."

Diggory Doo loves baseball,
and it's always been his dream
To learn to play it well
and to try out for a team.

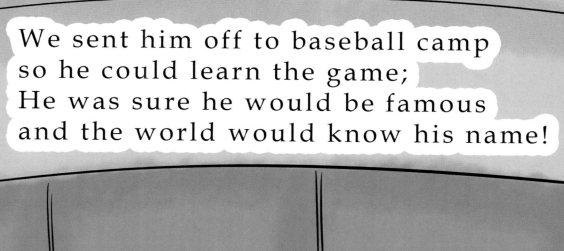

We sent him off to baseball camp
so he could learn the game;
He was sure he would be famous
and the world would know his name!

Although he looked quite spiffy in the uniform we bought, Diggory never listened to the lessons he was taught.

The coach told him what to do,
but Diggory never heard –
Instead of running towards first base,
Diggory ran to third!

Every time we tried
to help Diggory with a task,
He would snap, "I've got this!
If I need your help, I'll ask!"

After many failed attempts, Diggory Doo began to cry... "I always make a mess," he wailed. "I simply don't know why!"

"You've had the power within you to be successful all along"

"If you'd done as you were told,
things might not have turned out wrong."

"You're right; I've been hard headed,"
Diggory sadly sighed.
"If I'd followed the instructions,
I could have DONE the things I TRIED!"

So Diggory turned himself around
and changed that very day;
He said, "I'm going to listen
to what others have to say"

Read more about Drew and Diggory Doo!

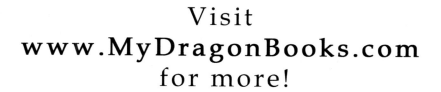

Visit
www.MyDragonBooks.com
for more!

Made in the USA
Columbia, SC
29 October 2021